PATHWAY TO THE STARS
playing for Alexa

David Turner

Rock's Mills Press
Rock's Mills, Ontario • Oakville, Ontario
2023

Published by

Rock's Mills Press

www.rocksmillspress.com

For information about this title, including permissions requests and
bulk sales orders, please contact the publisher at customer.service@
rocksmillspress.com.

for
Barbara, Constantine and Liam

Contents

Preface[1]

A ceremony and collage in two places, my home and the park just down the street that my dad initiated when he was on town council after retiring as managing editor of the Perth Courier.[2]

What more is there to say? Let me just play for Alexa.

David Turner,
Perth, Ontario
January 2023

1. "Scapes" via my Canon *PowerShot SX400 IS*.

2. Ironically, now that the park is primarily a place for exercise and relaxation, it is named "Last Duel Park" commemorating the last fatal duel in Canada when John Wilson shot Robert Lyon in a dispute over a woman's honour on June 13, 1833. However, being "the last" at least created a peaceful postscript.

I
PLAYING FOR ALEXA

I learned to play the *yiraga* or didjeridu in Australia during my time with the Aboriginal people of the Groote Eylandt archipelago between 1969 and 2003. My first music teacher was Jabeni Lalara who introduced *Life to the Power of N o t h i n g*.[1]

Back when I first arrived amongst the people, and on until the mid-1990s, it was not permitted to practice the *yiraga* in public—or even have someone teach you. You were supposed to learn by sitting with the adult players as a young man during ceremony, listening and watching over the years (only men play, women dance, the "reason" being simple: women embody a natural portal to "the other side" (*aiyugwarra mandja*, literally "the other side of water") and men do not; they compensate by "attaching" the *yiraga* to themselves). Nor could you play in public except during mortuary ceremonies. Nevertheless, Jabeni took pity on me and we occasionally headed into the bush for "lessons" with his son (below, note the stone in front of the end acting as an amplifier)—but this was only after I had learned the technique of circular breathing employed to play the instrument: snatch a breath of air through your nose, keep it under pressure in your cheeks, and then expel it through your mouth while holding that pressure, to produce a sound, then snatch another breath, and so on and so

1. Final edition, revised and expanded, published by Rock's Mills Press in 2023.

on. The effect is to play continuously from your diaphragm. This took some time to master:

I began by blowing bubbles with a straw in a glass of water, the reason being its small mouth which allowed me to contain the pressure in my cheeks. Then I graduated to a 2½-inch diameter PVC pipe as my containment strengthened. By 1993 I could carry a tune "chanting" the mouth-sound *degul-degul* into a full-sized *alabera,* or Stringybark, *yiraga* to achieve the proper tonguing which, together with the instrument's internal dynamics, produces some of its special overtone effects. Other effects, such as animal and bird sounds, could be voiced, as a rule not here during ceremony, but elsewhere in Aboriginal Australia.

Two rules I did learn early on: never hollow out the inside of the original cut wood to make or "improve" an instrument, and never let its mouth touch the ground once it is made.[1] Retaining the original cut wood allows the natural internal imperfections to remain which adds to the vibrancy of the instrument—that is, if you include termites as "natural" agents of the imperfections.

Sounds complicated but once you get the hang of it, it's not. What *is* complicated are the sounds themselves, particularly those you hear inside your head while playing. These are a fundamental note and three overtone-effects that simulate basic dimensions of the Cosmos as the Aborigines envision them: the real (*amamalya*), the "stuff" of original creation (Amawurrena), the Enveloping Lightness of Being surrounding all forms of Creation (Amawurrena of *awarrawalya*), and one's vital spirit (Amawurrena of *amugwa*). This suits its purpose, which, at least amongst the people I encountered in 1969, was to access another dimension of reality when someone died by detaching your

1. This is recounted in *Afterlife Before Genesis: Accessing the Eternal through Australian Aboriginal Music* (New York: Peter Lang Publishing, 1997).

Self from your self to aid another's Self in transitioning from the dimension into which he or she entered when they passed, and from there into another. This was accomplished both by the nature of the instrument, the way in which it was played, and the context in which it was played, namely during mortuary ceremonies.

Grief might prove debilitating at first and serve to clear the mind of all thoughts and distractions in preparation, except that the act of playing the *yiraga* induces a becalming state of mind/being in which only the sense of breathing remains. This is effected by the repetitive rhythms of the mouth-sound tempos (which there is no need to sound to oneself once one becomes adept at playing), of which there are three: *degul degul,* quick; *degul-degula-gula*, medium; and *degula degula*, slow. It is in a becalmed but empty state of mind/being that one potentially enters a mediating zone between the "real" and the "transcendent" and is able to open a portal for the departed in their journey.[1]

This was my experience playing for my dear friend and former partner Alexa when she passed. Alexa is mother to our son Liam, daughter to Barbara and Constantine Ponomareff. She met Jabeni and my mentor, Gula Lalara (Nawgulabena of the Warnungamadada), the most knowledgeable Songman in the Groote Eylandt archipelago, in 2003 as his health was declining, two years before he passed. (Photographs of both of us with him are included on the next page.)

1. The effects of the singing which *follows on* the sound of the *yiraga* and leads the spirit in its journey is another subject, one on which I am not qualified to comment except in principle, as I do not Sing. I imagine that following age-old Songlines, though, induces the same becalming effect as playing the *yiraga*. Again I refer to *Afterlife Before Genesis*.

Finding Her Way[1]

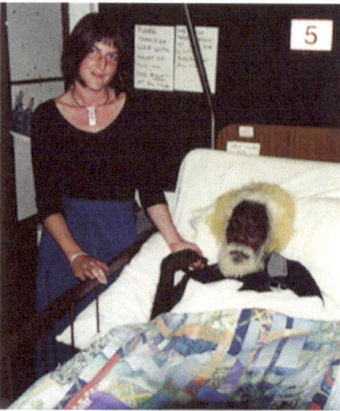

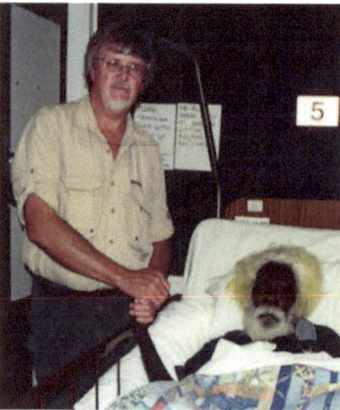

Alexa was diagnosed with cancer in March of 2020 and it was all over in seven weeks, just short of her 48th birthday (b. June 6, 1972). She died at her home on May 16th assisted by a doctor and she had asked me not to be present but to play for her at my place as my being there might upset the doctor. Other than the doctor, only her parents and Liam were present. Alexa said that she was afraid she wouldn't know where to go.

I had played with Gula and had the *yiraga* he had made and smoked for me in 1993. And I knew what to do.

By "smoked for me" I mean Gula had filled this *yiraga* with the Essential Nature (Amawurrena of *awarrawalya*)

of some of the most important places on Amagalyuagba, Bickerton Island. Connect to the Essential Natures of these Places by playing, and if all goes well, you open a portal that is "there and everywhere" in the eter-

1. Gratitude to Abbot Anshan Mohammad and the monks of Tisarana Monastery near Perth who dedicated their evening prayers to Alexa when she passed.

nal-now of the space-time continuum (my way of putting it).

Why did Gula smoke this one for me in the first place? It could only have been for me to use it.

I will simply recount what happened when I played for her ... in death ... after life ... before genesis ...as she might put it.

First the venue.

Gula's *yiraga* is on the right beside a small softwood (*mabunda*) decorative one, he made for me in 1969 into which he carved the Songs of the Lalara people. The one on the far left, from the Djowan people near Katherine in the Northern Territory, is my favourite

playing-for-fun one into which the artist has burned the image of the Essential Nature of the freshwater fish, Barramundi.[1] The ink painting of the meditating samurai and the vase are from Japan, a birthday present from Alexa during our visit there, and the two small figures of a shaman and a caribou in whalebone are by Piona Keyuakjuk[2] from

1. This *yiraga,* along with a number of others from my book *Afterlife Before Genesis,* I have recently passed on to Kyle Maplesden, retaining Gula's and two others. I seem to be losing touch with all but Gula's.

2. See my book *Eye of the Shaman: The Visions of Piona Keyuakjuk* (Oakville,

Pangnirtung on Baffin Island. Flanking these are ceremonial tapping sticks from Numbulwar on the mainland adjacent to Groote Eylandt gifted to me in 1969 by the principal songman of the Sacred Mardaiya:n ceremony. Upper left is an ink drawing of a Sage on rice paper, a birthday gift from my daughter Michelle.

May 16th, 2020

Woke up and went downstairs for some breakfast. Went outside on the deck and looked for my Dove (Derrarragugwa), which always seemed to appear when I did, but she was nowhere to be found. Then, as I was going inside, I turned and looked around and there she was perched on a branch on the tree to my right where I had "caught" her with my camera one day.

Today was an auspicious day. It was the day Alexa had decided to die. I was with Alexa for 12 years and when she recently asked me what the original attraction was, I replied "enigmatic, you appeared mysterious, different, unfathomable, as you remain."

Before she came down with cancer I hadn't played much at all and when she became ill I was recovering from a hernia operation and couldn't play without risk of compromising the incision. But after a month or so I decided to give it a go. I was rusty to say the least and started practicing, but rarely did I practice on Gula's instrument, which was for playing in ceremonies.

Ont.: Rock's Mills Press, 2018), which includes photographs of many of Piona's sculptures as well as his sketchbook drawings.

Though continuous playing without a break in the sound is possible with circular breathing, the Aboriginal tradition is to play continuously for short periods of anywhere from 30 seconds to a few minutes, usually accompanied by singing. The tapping sticks open each set to establish the rhythm and announce "we are coming over," then the *yiraga* enters, and finally the Song.

11:00 a.m–12:00 noon degul-degul

After 45 minutes on this rhythm (one of the three mouth-sounds employed), I began to see the sound emanating from the end of the instrument while the body of the *yiraga* before me began to disappear. (If you fully extend your right or left arm, then your fingers, while tucking you thumb under your hand, this will give you an idea of its Form.)

Then a 20-minute break, and I resumed.

12:20 p.m.–1:00 p.m. degul degul

Now, almost immediately, the sound appeared to me beyond the mouthpiece of the *yiraga*, and after about 15 minutes the body of the *yiraga* seemed to melt. Then to vanish, though never entirely.

Then another 20-minute break, and I resumed.

1:20 p.m.–2:00 p.m. *degul-degulagula*

My playing was becoming more fluid and relaxing as I went along. After about half-an-hour on this cadence with the sound appearing and the "melting" occurring, I heard a new "voice" in the instrument as I played: a kind of "pup" underneath the last *degul* as I pushed down on it in the transition to the opening *degul* of the next measure.

2:20 p.m.–3:00 p.m. *degula-degula*

About 20 minutes in, the sound began to disappear from

sight and the "melting" failed to occur. I had the sense that I was finished even though I continued playing. Was I getting tired as I had not played for this length of time for years, though I didn't feel tired? Or had I opened up a portal for Alexa's *amugwa* (vital spirit) to cross over to the other side? With no Song to accompany me and guide the *amugwa* I could not continue. And I had no idea at this point just at what moment her physical body had given up.

✳ ✳ ✳

The phone rang at 3:30. It was Liam asking me to come to Alexa's to pick him up. I came down the stairs and walked out to the deck to get some air. There on the same branch was a Dove. Turned around and walked out the front door to the car and there was a Dove on the wire that led from the post across the street to my house. I realized that it was the Essence of Dove, its Essential Nature, I was connected not to one Dove in particular—as in other traditions—but the Essential Nature of Derrarragugwa, one of my old friend Galiyawa Wurramarrba's Songs.[1]

It turned out that Alexa had passed away just after 11 a.m. Accounting for a period of "confusion" on her part, my efforts on her behalf, and what I had experienced while playing, this made sense.

The four strands of sound I had seen now and when I was playing with Gula reflected four dimensions of the Cosmos embodied within the *yiraga* and activated by the overtones generated by its playing, as I identified above.

1. *Life to the Power of N o t h i n g*, page 46.

Tidying Up

A week passed. The purpose of playing now was to "clean up" the "spiritual" residue (Amawurrena) of Alexa's living Presence and send it over to "her," a ceremony Aboriginal people also enacted after someone passed.

May 24th, 8:45 a.m.

Arrived at Alexa's home, lit my sage, and began smudging her car, inside and out. Then I proceeded indoors to the bathroom, kitchen, dining room, sun room, deck, and front porch. From there up to the spare room, back down to the basement and Liam's room, and finally up to Alexa's bedroom (below). There I smudged everything I could find, including the bed on which she had passed, then immediately opened a window, sat down on a wicker basket, and began to play—without Alexa in any form in mind as I had as she was dying. Now I was immersed in bits-and-pieces of her Amawurrena. They would "know" where to go.

9:30 a.m.–10:20 a.m.

I picked up the *degul-degul* rhythm quite quickly without the usual tuning-up period. I was feeling very relaxed and so, apparently, was Gula's *yiraga*. Quickly I began to slip into meditative mode.

The playing was easy, my mind was clear, and I became unusually aware of my breathing. Then the room in front of me began to fade except for my right hand holding the *yiraga*, my left holding a small stick to keep time on the instrument, and the *yiraga* before me. This impression continued through each set despite a momentary break until, finally, about half-an-hour later the room virtually vanished, but not my hands, the stick, and the *yiraga*. Then a soft white light began to appear around my hands, the stick, and the whole of the *yiraga*. Hands, stick, and *yiraga* now began to vanish with only the surrounding white light remaining which then began to stretch forward and funnel out from where the mouth of the *yiraga* had been.

I stopped playing. When I resumed, the experience did not continue, so I ended the session.

After relaxing for a few minutes, I began again on the *degul-degula-gula* rhythm, but whatever was done was done and I found myself just sitting there playing my *yiraga*. So after about another half an hour I brought it all to a close.

I had experienced the Amawurrena of *awarrawalya* of myself and my instruments, and … an absence[1] … so I knew the residue of her Being had found its way as …? to where …? *Aiyugwarra mandj*a, "the other side" (literally, of water). To her archetypal "force for Forming" from which each of us originated? Or another?

In strictly Aboriginal terms, the preconditions for effecting a transition were there: Amawurrena of *awarrawalya* connections between Alexa and myself and the *yiraga*'s connection to the special places on Amagaluagba, in turn connected to the "other side of this side" and the "archetypal Forms," or forces for Forming, in the Cos-

---

1. What else can I call it except "N o t h i n g," which might create the impression of an all-encompassing dimension which *i t* is not. "It" as conventionally written? You see the problem. And "see"? If you "saw" there wouldn't be a problem.

mos[1]—which give birth to every thing that each of us, and every thing in Creation, is.[2]

1 *Life to the Power of N o t h i n g*, I.

2. Songs are by their Essential Nature connected to the "other side of this side," the singer in ceremony requiring an Amawurrena of *awarrawalya* connection to the deceased and the *yiraga* player(s) in order to "cross over."

II
LIFE

III
SUNRISE[1]

1. June 4th, 2022.

IV
SUNRISEN[1]

1. June 5th, 2022.

Acknowledgement

Teachings
from Life and Death

1. Life's too short so lengthen it, by collapsing it into the moment, and
2. Look for the best in people and you will see it. Look for the worst and that's all you will see.
3. Tell someone about the best you see in them and they will see it as well.
4. Tell someone about the worst you see in them and …
5. "Competition rather than money is the root of all evil."—Glenn Gould
6. No "yes-buts"—only "both-ands."
7. Give without expectation of return, receive and give to another.
8. Compassion, not colour or gender, is the measure of a person.
9. "There are more things in Heaven and Earth, Horatio, than are dreamt of in your philosophy."—Shakespeare
10. Death is the full emptiment of a life … and …
11. Wiyaw (goodbye and hello at the same time).

www.ingramcontent.com/pod-product-compliance
Lightning Source LLC
Chambersburg PA
CBHW040934030426
42337CB00001B/11